Forgotten Victims

The Genocide of the Roma and Sinti

Barbara Warnock

**The Wiener
Holocaust Library**

Exhibition 30 October 2019 – 11 March 2020

The Wiener Holocaust Library
29 Russell Square
London WC1B 5DP

Introduction

The genocide carried out against the Romani and Sinti communities of Europe by the Nazis and their collaborators during the Second World War – the persecution and murder of as many as 500,000 people – has been referred to as 'the forgotten Holocaust'.

After the war, survivors and the relatives of victims struggled to get recognition and compensation for the persecution and losses they had suffered. In Britain and Europe today, prejudice and discrimination against Roma, Gypsies and Travellers are still common.

This exhibition and catalogue draw upon The Wiener Holocaust Library's collections of material on the genocide against the Roma to uncover the stories of this lesser-known aspect of Nazi persecution.

Since the 1950s, the Library has collected documents about the persecution of Roma and Sinti, including eyewitness accounts and documents from the earliest systematic research project into the genocide, undertaken in the 1960s by Donald Kenrick and Grattan Puxon.

The genocide against the Roma can be defined as a part of the Holocaust. Sometimes, however, the term Holocaust is used only to mean the systematic murder of six million European Jews between 1941 and 1945.

Various Romani terms have been used to describe the Roma Genocide, including *Porajmos, Pharrajimos* and *Samudaripen*, but no one term has been commonly agreed.

Photograph of a Roma man, thought to be Jozef Kwiek, in Belzec concentration camp in German-occupied Poland, 1940
Wiener Holocaust Library Collections

Roma lives

Roma (or Romani) people left northern India perhaps about a thousand years ago. They arrived in central Europe by around the early fifteenth century. Roma are a diverse people. Some Roma are Christians and some are Muslims. Roma speak dialects of Romani, a language based upon the classical Indian language of Sanskrit.

Roma is the term used to include a range of groups who share a common heritage and language –Romani. The term is used to describe Roma, a group from Eastern Europe and the Balkans; Sinti from Germany, France and Northern Italy; Lalleri from Czech lands; Kale from Finland, Wales, Spain and Portugal, and Manouches from France and Italy.

Roma and Traveller communities have historically been referred to as 'Gypsies' in Britain and as *Zigeuner* in Germany.

The term 'Gypsy' emerged from a mistaken belief that Roma had come to Europe from Egypt. The word *Zigeuner* may derive from a term meaning 'untouchable' and reflects the history of prejudice and discrimination faced by Roma in Europe.

There is a high degree of uncertainty about the size of the Roma population in Europe prior to the Second World War. Particularly sizeable communities were based in Romania, Yugoslavia, the USSR, Hungary and Bulgaria.

Many Roma were self-employed, traditionally as metalworkers, craftsmen, toolmakers, cobblers and horse-traders. Others worked as musicians, dancers or in circuses.

By the twentieth century, some Roma in Europe lived in settled homes. Many German Roma and Sinti were assimilated into German society and were employed in a wide range of fields, including shop-keeping and in administrative positions.

Photograph depicting the visit of three Sinti women, including Erna Lauenburger (first left) to Hanns Weltzel's house. Weltzel's wife Klara is pictured second left, photograph by Hanns Weltzel, c.mid-1930s
By courtesy of Liverpool University Library, GLS Add GA 3/2/49

Hans Braun

> I am a Gypsy (*Zigeuner*). I was born in Hannover, Germany, in 1923. They called me *Haeschen*, little rabbit, probably because I hopped around so much as a young child. My immediate family consisted of my father, mother and eleven children, three brothers and eight sisters. We travelled around in a horse-drawn wagon. We had a small carnival with swings, a merry-go-round, shooting gallery, etc. We travelled around the countryside all summer long, and in the winter we stayed at our home base. We were all born in Germany, we were all German Gypsies (Sinti).

From 'A Sinti Survivor Speaks': Hans Braun's account of his childhood, translated by Hannah Silver. Wiener Holocaust Library Collections

Braun was a German Sinti man born in Hannover in 1923. At the start of the war, he was forced into labour in a munitions factory for the German state. In 1941, his machine broke: this made him liable for arrest by the Gestapo. Braun then lived in hiding and on the run in Germany and in Luxembourg, except for a brief period of incarceration (from which he escaped). He was finally arrested in Luxembourg and sent to Auschwitz-Birkenau, where he was reunited with his family. Braun was transferred to Flossenbürg concentration camp in Bavaria in late 1944 to work as a slave labourer. Most of Braun's family died in Auschwitz of illness, starvation or gassing.

Braun attempted to claim compensation from the German government after the war.

Prejudice and discrimination against Roma before the Nazi era

Prejudice, discrimination and hostility against Roma and Travellers were widespread in Europe for centuries before the Nazi era. In the nineteenth century, many anti-Roma measures remained in place, even as Jews were emancipated. During this time many regions of Germany passed new anti-Roma laws.

In Weimar-era Germany (1919-1933), a law, *Combatting Gypsies, Vagabonds and the Work Shy*, was passed in Bavaria in 1926. It required all Sinti and Roma to register with the police and other public bodies. Arbitrary arrests of Roma were common. In 1929, these regulations were adopted by the German national police force. In the same year, the Bavarian police set up the *Centre for the Fight Against Gypsies in Germany*.

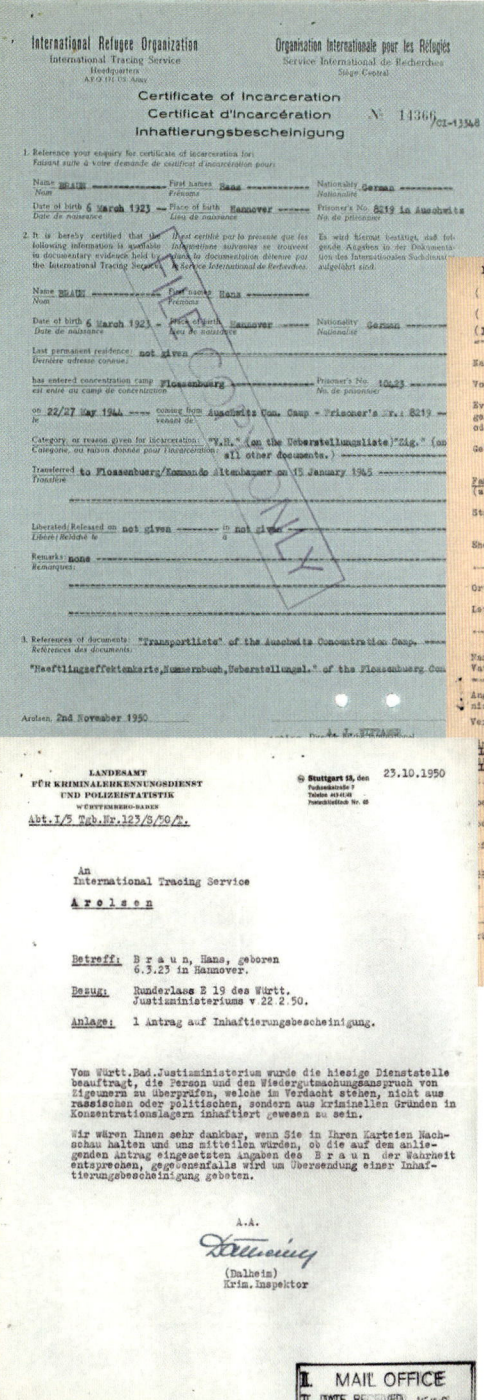

Hans Braun's Certificate of Incarceration confirming that he had been a prisoner in Auschwitz and Flossenbürg, 1950
Doc. No 1101269562

Hans Braun's second application for restitution from the German government, 1956 Doc. No 101269554

A letter about Hans Braun from a criminal investigator with the German police to the International Tracing Service in Arolsen, 1950
Doc No 101269560

Inspector Dalheim asked the International Tracing Service whether they could confirm that Hans Braun was not held in Auschwitz and Flossenbürg for 'racial' or 'political' reasons, but because he was a criminal. Dalheim's enquiry was made as a result of Braun's first restitution claim. Sinti and Roma were often prevented from claiming restitution in the 1940s and 1950s because of spurious accusations that they were not incarcerated for 'racial' reasons.

All images © International Tracing Service Digital Archive, Wiener Holocaust Library Collections

Nazi persecution of Roma and Sinti 1933-1939

Persecution of Roma and Sinti intensified in Germany after the Nazi accession to power in January 1933.

Roma were not central to the Nazis' racist world view in the way that Jews were, but they too were regarded as 'of alien blood' and a threat to the racial strength of the 'Aryan master race'.

Roma and Sinti were often targeted in Nazi Germany in the 1930s for exhibiting allegedly anti-social behaviour, such as vagrancy. For the Nazis, those labelled anti-social (in German, *Asoziale*), were usually by definition racially threatening, their 'undesirable' characteristics indicating racial inferiority.

By the mid-1930s, the Nazis had banned Roma and Sinti from working in certain occupations, and Sinti and Roma became targets for forced sterilisation aimed at preventing their continuation as a group. A large number of Sinti and Roma were forced to live in special internment camps.

After the German takeover of Austria (the *Anschluss*) in March 1938, the threat to Austrian Roma increased.

Over a thousand Roma and Sinti in Germany and Austria were arrested and sent to concentration camps such as Dachau in June 1938. Some had failed to register a permanent address, as required by the 1937 *Decree on the Fight to Prevent Crime*. Others were arrested arbitrarily as part of an intensification of anti-Roma action that followed Heydrich's order of June 1938. Killings of Roma and Sinti and other so-called 'a-social' prisoners began in camps like Mauthausen before the start of the war.

Roma prisoners in Dachau concentration camp, 20 June 1938
Bundesarchiv, Bild 152-27-11a / Friedrich Bauer

Hermine Horvath

> We had no rights in any aspect of our lives. We could no longer attend school. We could only go shopping in the hours between 11:00 and 12:00. We could not go to any dances, cinemas, or any public events. In short we were outcasts. I was then 13 years old.

Hermine Horvath, a Roma woman from Burgenland in Austria, described the situation for her family after the German takeover of Austria in March 1938. Her father was deported to Dachau concentration camp in June 1938. Horvath gave her testimony to The Wiener Library's eyewitness account project. Her account is remarkable for its candour about her experiences of sexual violence. She speaks of one occasion in Austria in the late 1930s, when an SS man in whose farm she was a forced labourer threatened her:

> I noticed very quickly that this [local SS leader] did not worry at all about the Racial Problem when it came to a young Gypsy girl. He started to come after me... One day he was suddenly standing in front of me with a drawn pistol.

Later, following her deportation to Auschwitz-Birkenau in 1943, Horvath recounted that 'it was especially terrible for us that we had the SS men staring at us in our undressed state all the time. One SS squad leader in Block 8 took women whenever and wherever it suited him.'

She also describes the rape and murder of two gypsy children by an SS officer in Auschwitz.

Horvath died at 33 shortly after this testimony was given, likely as a result of the privations she had suffered as a camp inmate, slave labourer and victim of forced experimentation.

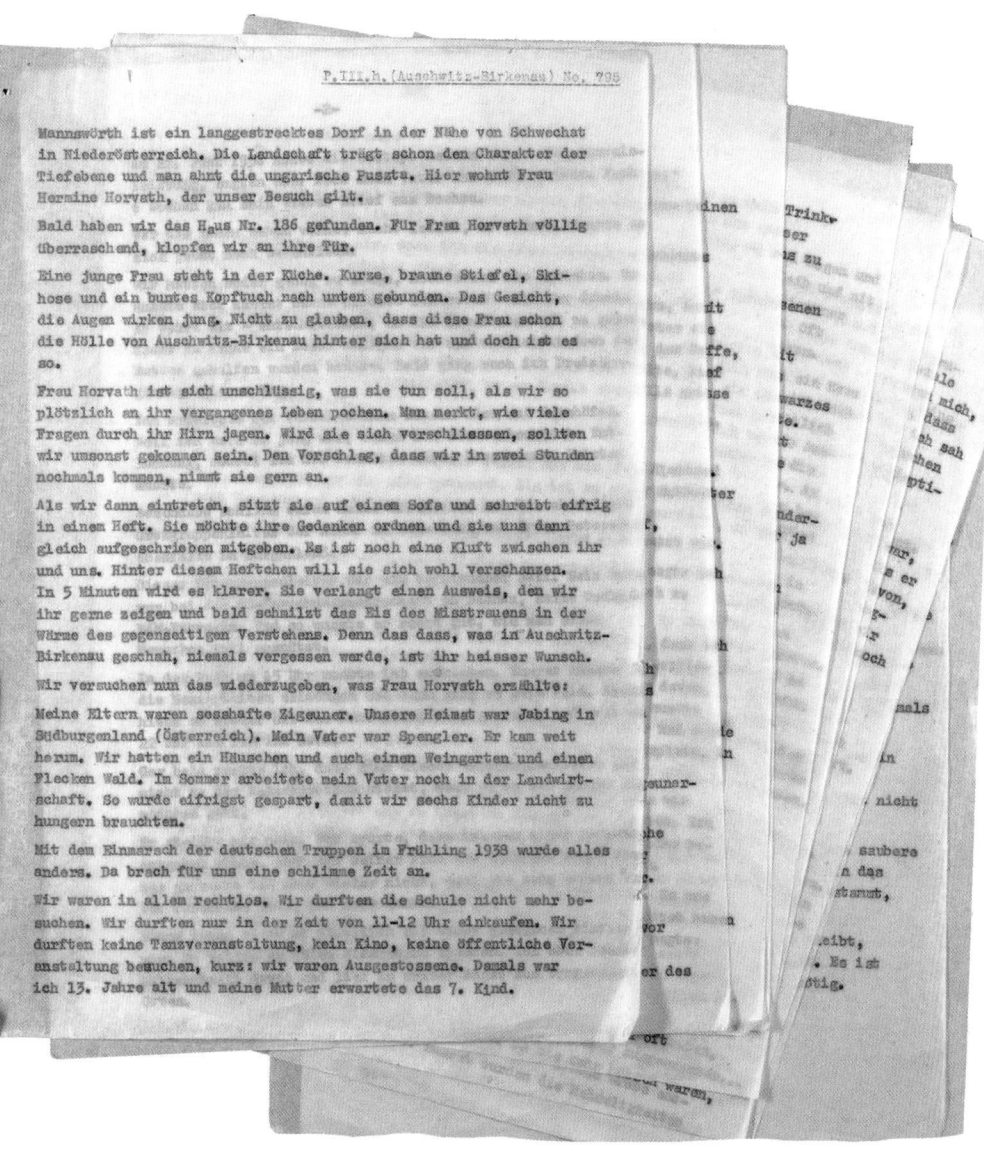

P.III.h.(Auschwitz-Birkenau) No. 795

Mannswörth ist ein langgestrecktes Dorf in der Nähe von Schwechat in Niederösterreich. Die Landschaft trägt schon den Charakter der Tiefebene und man ahnt die ungarische Puszta. Hier wohnt Frau Hermine Horvath, der unser Besuch gilt.

Bald haben wir das Haus Nr. 186 gefunden. Für Frau Horvath völlig überraschend, klopfen wir an ihre Tür.

Eine junge Frau steht in der Küche. Kurze, braune Stiefel, Skihose und ein buntes Kopftuch nach unten gebunden. Das Gesicht, die Augen wirken jung. Nicht zu glauben, dass diese Frau schon die Hölle von Auschwitz-Birkenau hinter sich hat und doch ist es so.

Frau Horvath ist sich unschlüssig, was sie tun soll, als wir so plötzlich an ihr vergangenes Leben pochen. Man merkt, wie viele Fragen durch ihr Hirn jagen. Wird sie sich verschliessen, sollten wir umsonst gekommen sein. Den Vorschlag, dass wir in zwei Stunden nochmals kommen, nimmt sie gern an.

Als wir dann eintreten, sitzt sie auf einem Sofa und schreibt eifrig in einem Heft. Sie möchte ihre Gedanken ordnen und sie uns dann gleich aufgeschrieben mitgeben. Es ist noch eine Kluft zwischen ihr und uns. Hinter diesem Heftchen will sie sich wohl verschanzen. In 5 Minuten wird es klarer. Sie verlangt einen Ausweis, den wir ihr gerne zeigen und bald schmilzt das Eis des Misstrauens in der Wärme des gegenseitigen Verstehens. Denn das dass, was in Auschwitz-Birkenau geschah, niemals vergessen werde, ist ihr heisser Wunsch.

Wir versuchen nun das wiederzugeben, was Frau Horvath erzählte:

Meine Eltern waren sesshafte Zigeuner. Unsere Heimat war Jabing in Südburgenland (Österreich). Mein Vater war Spengler. Er kam weit herum. Wir hatten ein Häuschen und auch einen Weingarten und einen Flecken Wald. Im Sommer arbeitete mein Vater noch in der Landwirtschaft. So wurde eifrigst gespart, damit wir sechs Kinder nicht zu hungern brauchten.

Mit dem Einmarsch der deutschen Truppen im Frühling 1938 wurde alles anders. Da brach für uns eine schlimme Zeit an.

Wir waren in allem rechtlos. Wir durften die Schule nicht mehr besuchen. Wir durften nur in der Zeit von 11-12 Uhr einkaufen. Wir durften keine Tanzveranstaltung, kein Kino, keine öffentliche Veranstaltung besuchen, kurz: wir waren Ausgestossene. Damals war ich 13. Jahre alt und meine Mutter erwartete das 7. Kind.

The testimony of Hermine Horvath with translation, collected in Vienna in 1958 as part of The Wiener Library's project to gather eyewitness accounts of the Holocaust
Wiener Holocaust Library Collections

> Leseabschrift
>
> REICHSKRIMINALPOLIZEIAMT   Berlin, am 1. Juni 1938
> Tgb.Nr. RKPA 6001/295.38
>
> SCHNELLBRIEF!
>
> STRENG VERTRAULICH
>
> An die
> Staatliche Kriminalpolizei
> Kriminalpolizeileitstelle
> in ....
>
> Betrifft: Vorbeugende Verbrechungsbekämpfung durch die
> Polizei
>
> Da das Verbrechertum im Asozialen seine Wurzeln hat und sich fortlaufend aus ihm ergänzt, hat der Erlass des RuPrMdJ. v. 14. Dezember 1937 - Pol. ..../37 - 2098 - der Kriminalpolizei weitgehende Möglichlichkeiten gegeben, neben den Berufsverbrechern auch alle asozialen Elemente zu erfassen, die durch ihr Verhalten der Gemeinschaft zur Last fallen und sie dadurch schädigen. Ich habe aber feststellen müssen, daß der Erlass bisher nicht mit der erforderlichen Schärfe zur Anwendung gebracht worden ist.
> Die straffe Durchführung des Vierteljahresplanes erfordert den Einsatz aller arbeitsfähigen Kräfte und läßt es nicht zu, daß asoziale Menschen sich der Arbeit entziehen und somit den Vierjahresplan sabotieren.
> Ich ordne deshalb an:
> 1. Ohne Rücksicht auf die bereits vom Geheimen Staatspolizeiamt im März d.J. durchgeführte Sonderaktion gegen Asoziale und unter schärfster Anwendung des Erlasses vom 14. Dezember 1937 in der Woche vom 13. bis 18. Juni 1938 aus dem dortigen Kriminalpolizeileitstellenbezirke mindestens 200 männliche arbeitsfähige Personen (asoziale) in polizeiliche Vorbeugungshaft zu nehmen. Dabei sind vor allem zu berücksichtigen
>   a) Landstreicher, die zur Zeit ohne Arbeit von Ort zu Ort ziehen;

The June 1938 '*Asoziale*' Directive, issued by Reinhard Heydrich,
Head of the Reich Security Police
International Tracing Service Archive, Wiener Holocaust Library Collections, Doc No 82342397

A decree in December 1937 allowed for the arbitrary arrest and detention of 'antisocials'. This June 1938 directive, issued by Heydrich to the Criminal Police in Germany, ordered the arbitrary arrest and detention of 'antisocials', specifically the 'workshy'. Heydrich justified this on the basis that 'criminality has its roots in antisocials'. He defined 'antisocials' as including 'Gypsies and people moving about in a Gypsy-like way if they have not shown any intention to work or have become criminal', along with 'beggars' and 'tramps'. The *Asoziale* directive led to widespread arrests of Roma.

Photograph of Nazi 'race scientist' Robert Ritter (right), taking a blood sample from a Romani or Sinti woman, c.1936-1940
Bundesarchiv, R 165 Bild-244-70

'Racial-biological research'
Dr Robert Ritter led the Racial Hygiene and Demographic Biology Research Unit from 1936. He was also head of a Criminal Biology Unit attached to the police force from 1941. He conducted 'research' to try to identify supposed 'racial' characteristics of Roma and Sinti, and to try to show that Roma were 'racially' inferior. He was particularly concerned to prevent intermarriage between Roma and Sinti and other Germans. He also supported the policy of sterilising Roma and Sinti women and later was the leading figure who worked to identify Roma and Sinti who were then arrested and deported to camps.

> Experience gained in combating the Gypsy nuisance, and knowledge derived from race-biological research, have shown that the proper method of attacking the Gypsy problem seems to be to treat it as a matter of race. It has... become necessary to distinguish between pure and part-Gypsies in the final solution of the Gypsy question. Treatment of the Gypsy question is part of the National Socialist task of national regeneration.
>
> Translated extracts from Head of SS Heinrich Himmler's circular, *Combatting the Gypsy Nuisance*, 8 December 1938

The 'racial-biological research' mentioned by Heinrich Himmler was the kind of research undertaken by Robert Ritter and his associates. Roma and Sinti were of particular interest to Nazi 'race' scientists, and often subjected to forced medical experiments.

ANORDNUNG

des Kreishauptmanns von Minsk Maz. ueber Aufenthaltsverbot fuer Zigeuner.

Auf Grund der §§ 1 und 2 der Verordnung über Aufenthaltsbeschränkungen im Generalgouvernement vom 13. September 1940. (VBlGG. I S. 288) ordne ich folgendes an:

Zigeunern wird mit sofortiger Wirkung der Aufenthalt im Kreise Minsk-Maz. bis auf weiteres verboten.

Sämtliche im Kreise Minsk-Maz. wohnhaften Zigeuner haben sich unter Vorlage ihrer Ausweispapiere beim Kreishauptmann in Minsk Maz., Zimmer 26, zu melden.

Zuwiderhandelnde werden mit Geldstrafe bis zu 1000.- zl. im Nichtbeitreibungsfalle mit Haft bis zu drei Monaten bestraft.

Minsk Maz., den 9. Dezember 1940.

Der Kreishauptmann
Dr. BITTRICH

ZARZĄDZENIE

Starosty na powiat Minsk Maz. dotyczące zakazu przebywania dla cyganów.

Na podstawie § 1 i 2 Rozporządzenia z dnia 13 września 1940. (VBl GG I S. 288) dotyczącego ograniczeń pobytu na terenie Generalnej Guberni zarządzam co następuje:

Niniejszym zakazuje się cyganom przebywania na terenie powiatu mińsko-mazowieckiego aż do odwołania.

Wszyscy zamieszkali w powiecie cyganie winni natychmiast zgłosić się w Starostwie, pokój 26. Należy przedłożyć równocześnie dowody osobiste.

Wykroczenie przeciw powyższemu zarządzeniu karane będzie grzywną do 1000.- zł. a w razie nieściągalności aresztem do 3 miesięcy.

Mińsk-Maz., dnia 9. grudnia 1940.

Starosta Powiatu
Dr. BITTRICH

War 1939-1941

The start of the Second World War saw an escalation in Nazi oppression against Roma and Sinti. Across Europe millions of Jews and Roma faced persecution, deportations to ghettos and camps and then genocide, as the German army invaded Poland (1939), the Low Countries and France (1940).

German and Austrian Roma and Sinti who were not deported endured confinement, forced labour, medical experiments and the threat of forced sterilisations.

Alsatian Romani in Rivesaltes internment / transit camp, c.1941-1942
United States Holocaust Memorial Museum, courtesy of Friedel Bohny-Reiter
By courtesy of Liverpool University Library, GLS Add GA 3/2/49

> The genocide against the Roma had many similarities with the genocide carried out against the Jews of Europe at the same time. Roma were targeted for persecution and murder on 'racial' grounds, just as Jews were. Roma experienced arrests, deportation, incarceration, forced and slave labour, maltreatment and murder in camps, and murder by mass shooting across central and Eastern Europe.
>
> German and Austrian Roma and Sinti were also subject to a massive programme of pseudo-scientific investigation and sterilisation, and those of mixed Roma and 'German' descent were regarded as a threat to German racial purity. Others died of starvation and disease after forced deportations. Roma were not central to Nazi racist ideology in the way that Jews were and the implementation of persecution against them was more haphazard and inconsistent than that against Europe's Jews.

A copy of an order in German and Polish issued by the German authorities in Mińsk Mazowiecki in occupied Poland, 9 December 1940. The order banned itinerant Roma from the town and ordered settled Roma to register with the authorities
International Tracing Service Archive, Wiener Holocaust Library Collections, Doc No 82342405

Kurt Ansin

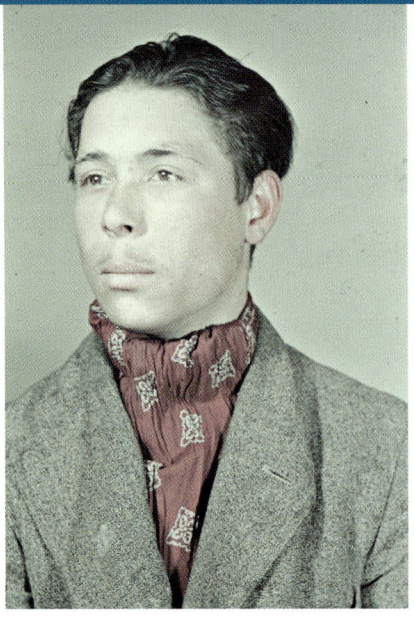

Kurt Ansin, c.1940
Bundesarchiv, Bild R 165-88

Kurt Ansin (1921-1984) and his family were forced to live in the 'Gypsy Camp' in Magdeburg. In 1938 he was deported to Buchenwald concentration camp in central Germany and later to the Auschwitz concentration camp complex, where most of his family were murdered. In 1944, he was transferred to Buchenwald concentration camp and then Mittelbau-Dora as a slave labourer. After the war, Ansin settled in East Berlin and gave his testimony about his experiences to Donald Kenrick.

Camp for Roma in Łódź, c.1940-1944
United States Holocaust Memorial Museum, courtesy of Robert Adams

From May 1940, German Roma and Sinti started to be deported to ghettos in Poland. In autumn 1941, 5,000 Austrian Roma were sent to the Jewish ghetto in Łódź. They were then deported to Chełmno death camp where they were one of the first groups to be murdered by gas.

Theresia Reinhardt

Theresia Reinhardt was a Sinti woman and a dancer at The Würzburg State Opera in Germany. Along with the other female members of her family, she was forced to sign papers to authorise her sterilisation. Reinhardt decided to try to get pregnant. By the time her sterilisation appointment was scheduled, she was three months pregnant. She was allowed to proceed with her pregnancy but she and her boyfriend, later husband, Gabriel, were monitored throughout.

Their twins, Rolanda and Rita, were removed from their parents at birth and taken to a clinic and subjected to horrific medical experimentation. Rolanda died in the course of an experiment.

After the war, Theresia Reinhardt and her daughter Rita ran a Sinti organisation in West Germany that campaigned for recognition of the genocide against Sinti and Roma.

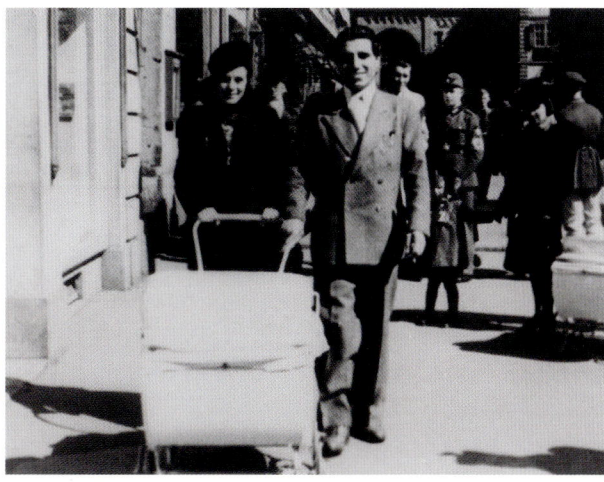

Theresia Reinhardt

Theresia Reinhardt and her husband Gabriel push their twins, Rolanda and Rita in Würzburg under Nazi escort, 1943

Rita Reinhardt in 1948

All images United States Holocaust Memorial Museum, courtesy Rita Prigmore

Nazi persecution of Roma and Sinti Central and Western Europe

From early 1942, Nazi persecution against the Roma escalated, as thousands of the German and Austrian Sinti and Roma who had been confined to ghettos in Poland were deported to Chełmno and Treblinka death camps and murdered by gas.

In late 1942, head of the *Schutzstaffel* (SS, the Nazi organisation in charge of 'racial' policy and the Holocaust), Heinrich Himmler, ordered most remaining Sinti and Roma be deported from Greater Germany to camps in occupied Poland.

In Auschwitz-Birkenau a specific section of the camp, B II e, was designated the '*Zigeunerlager*' ('Gypsy' camp), in 1943. German, Austrian and other Roma and Sinti were later deported there. Around 23,000 Roma and Sinti were ultimately held in Auschwitz, of whom 21,000 were murdered.

In an Eyewitness Report of the 'Gypsy' Camp at Auschwitz Hermann Langbein in 1945 recounted:

> The conditions were worse than in other camps... In April 1943 I was outside, and I saw the following. The route between the huts was ankle deep in mud and dirt. The gypsies were still wearing the clothes that they had been given upon arrival... footwear was missing... The latrines were built in such a way that they were practically unusable for the gypsy children. The infirmary was a pathetic sight.

On 2-3 August 1944, on Heinrich Himmler's orders, the 'Gypsy' Camp at Auschwitz-Birkenau was liquidated. Despite determined resistance from the Roma in the camp, all 2,897 remaining inhabitants were murdered in gas chambers.

August, a Sinti boy (centre), son of Wiena Ansin, and relatives photographed by Hanns Weltzel, Germany, c.1933-1937. One of the other children was likely called Sonja Laúbinger. August and Sonja died in Auschwitz, as almost certainly did the other child.
By courtesy of the University of Liverpool Library, GLS Add GA 1/2

László Stoika

László Stoika (b.1941) was deported by Hungarian authorities from Budapest to Dachau concentration camp with his parents and two older brothers in November 1944. The children and their mother were transferred to Bergen-Belsen, where they were liberated. Their mother died not long after liberation due to ill health. The boys were sent to hospital to recuperate. While László remained in a hospital in Germany, his elder brothers were repatriated to Hungary. He was taken to a United Nations Relief and Rehabilitation Administration (UNRRA) children's centre and then to Switzerland for six months for recuperation.

Post-war relief agencies tried to trace his father, who was last seen in Dachau, to no avail. László was deemed ineligible for immigration to the United States, because of his mental and physical condition.

László was repatriated to Hungary in 1950 to his grandmother, who had custody of one of his brothers.

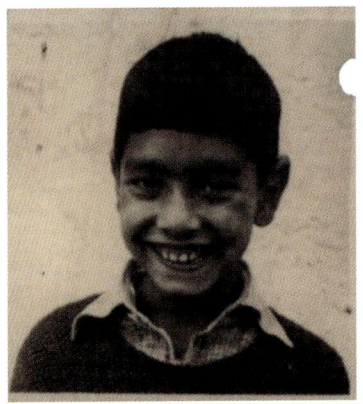

László Stoika, undated, c. late 1940s
International Tracing Service Archive, Wiener Holocaust Library Collections, Doc No 84523672

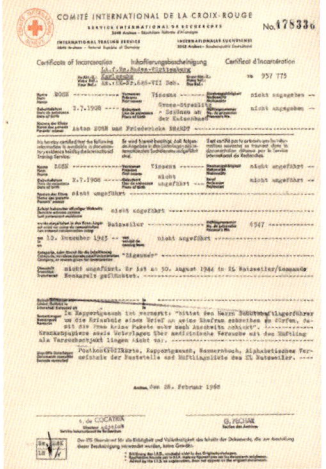

Hungarian Red Cross Letter about László Stoika, 5 February 1948.
International Tracing Service Archive, Wiener Holocaust Library Collections, Doc No 84523719

The Hungarian Red Cross helped facilitate the repatriation and reunion, despite its unfavourable assessment of the grandmother's ability to care for László. The Hungarian Red Cross letter demonstrates the persistence of anti-gypsyism into the post-war period.

Vinzenz Rose

Vinzenz Rose (1908-1996), a Sinti man, ran a cinema in Darmstadt with his parents and brother. The cinema was forced out of business by the Nazis in 1937 for 'racial' reasons.

From 1940 to 1943, Rose lived on the run or under false identities in Germany and Czechoslovakia. In 1943, his family was denounced and Rose was arrested by the Gestapo.

He was deported to the Gypsy Camp in Auschwitz-Birkenau.

After a few weeks, he was transferred to the main camp at Auschwitz and then to Natzweiler-Struthof concentration camp in Germany. There he was a slave labourer and endured forced medical experiments. In April 1944, he was transferred to Neckarelz, a satellite camp of Natzweiler, from where he managed to escape.

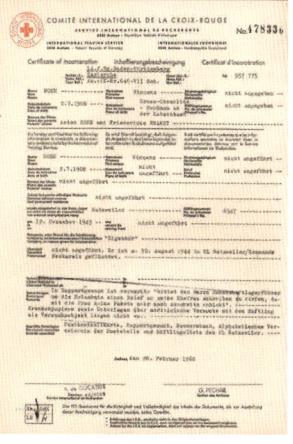

A post-war Red Cross certificate about Vinzenz Rose's incarceration
© International Tracing Service Digital Archive, Wiener Holocaust Library Collections, Doc No 109105650

This certificate shows that Rose was incarcerated in Natzweiler because he was a *Zigeuner* (Gypsy), and that he was not transferred or released but *geflüchtet* (escaped) from the camp.

Photograph at Auschwitz of an unknown Roma or Sinti victim of Nazi persecution, date unknown
Wiener Holocaust Library Collections

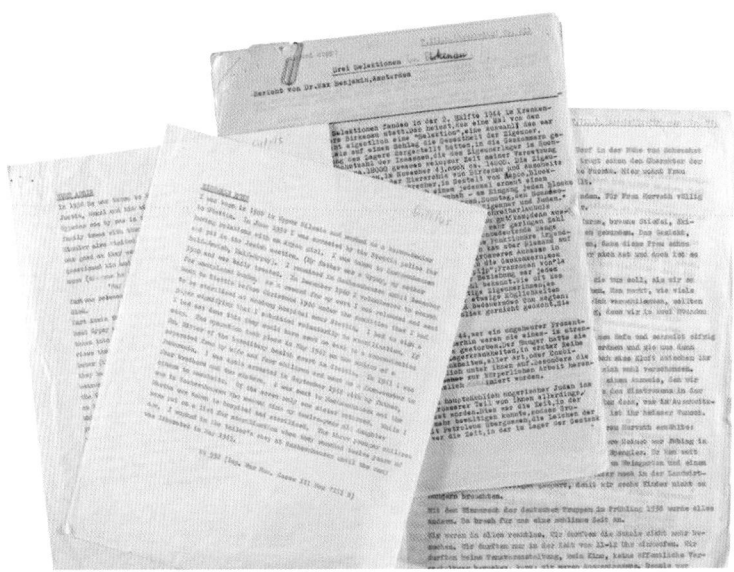

Eyewitness accounts of the genocide against the Roma, and summaries of survivor testimonies
Wiener Holocaust Library Collections

The Wiener Holocaust Library has a number of accounts given by survivors of the genocide against the Roma, collected as part of its project, launched in the 1950s, to gather eyewitness accounts of the Holocaust from across Europe. Hermine Horvath (see pages 12-13) gave her testimony as part of this project. Seen above is the testimony of Julius Hodosi, collected in 1957. Hodosi was a Roma man from Burgenland in Austria. He volunteered for the German Army after the *Anschluss* of 1938, but was expelled because he was Romani. In 1941, he and his wife were arrested and sent to Lackenbach camp, where they were mistreated by the SS. Ultimately, the couple were deported to Auschwitz-Birkenau. In this account, Hodosi describes the horrendous conditions of the 'Gypsy' Camp at Auschwitz: his two daughters starved to death there.

The Library's eyewitness reports collections also include accounts given by Jewish survivors and others that describe aspects of the persecution and genocide directed against Europe's Roma population by the Nazis and their collaborators. Examples of these include a report pictured above by Dr. Max Benjamin of the murder of the inhabitants 'Gypsy' Camp in Auschwitz on 2-3 August 1944. Benjamin was a doctor at the 'Gypsy' Hospital in Auschwitz. He was a Jew from Cologne who was also incarcerated in Auschwitz. He gave his account to The Wiener Library in 1958.

Also pictured above are some summaries of accounts by Roma survivors collected by Donald Kenrick and Grattan Puxon in the 1960s. Their project was the first attempt to conduct comprehensive research into the persecution of Roma in the Nazi era. It was in part funded by the Institute for Contemporary History, as the Wiener Holocaust Library was then known.

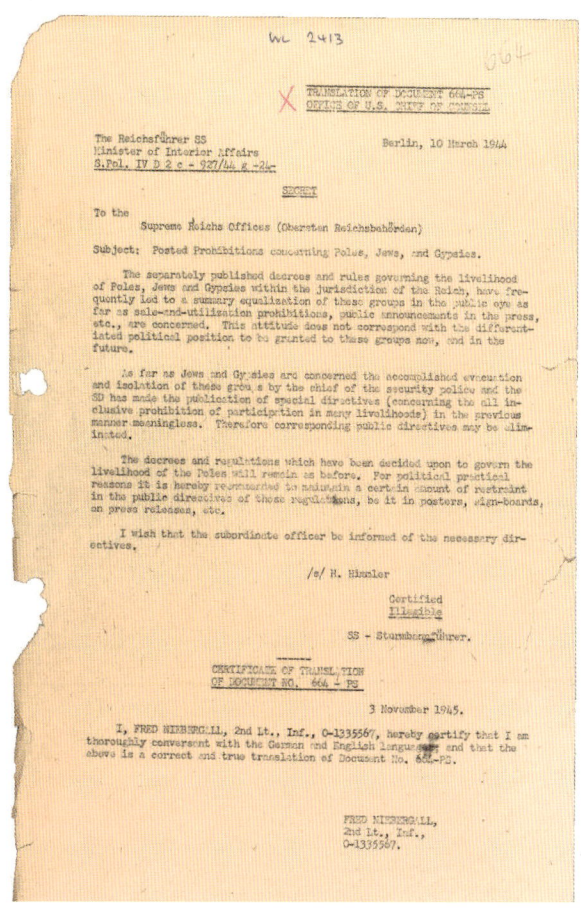

Heinrich Himmler, 'Posted Prohibitions Concerning Poles, Jews, and Gypsies', 10 March 1944
A translation from the Nuremburg War Crimes trial documents, Wiener Holocaust Library Collections

In this document from 1944, Himmler noted that 'the accomplished evacuation and isolation' of Jews and Gypsies meant that directives against them were no longer necessary. 'Evacuation' and 'isolation' meant that the vast majority of Jews, Sinti and Roma from greater Germany had been deported to ghettos and camps and murdered.

Estonia

Latvia

Lithuania

Soviet Union

In the **Soviet Union** and the Baltic States of **Lithuania**, **Latvia** and **Estonia**, the *Einsatzgruppen* and their collaborators murdered tens of thousands of Roma, who were often labelled as 'spies' and 'saboteurs' by the Nazis.

In the **Crimea** (a part of the Ukrainian Soviet Socialist Republic), Jews, Crimchaks (a Jewish ethno-religious community) and Roma were targeted for murder by the Nazis and their collaborators.

In **Hungary** in 1944 and 1945, many Roma were forced into labour. Others were deported to German camps or massacred.

Hungary

Croatia

Serbia

Romania

Crimea

In **Romania** between 1942 and 1944, the pro-Nazi Antonescu regime deported more than 26,000 Romanian Roma to Transnistria.

In **Croatia**, the fascist Ustaše conducted ruthless persecution against local Roma populations. Roma were deported to labour camps and the Jasenovac concentration camp. In Jasenovac, most Roma were murdered shortly after arrival. Between 10,000 and 20,000 Roma were killed in Jasenovac.

Serbia was under direct German military administration from April 1941. Roma there were subject to murder in retaliation for the killing of German Army (*Wehrmacht*) soldiers by Yugoslav Partisans. There were also massacres of Roma carried out in special camps, and murders in mobile gas vans.

The Genocide against Roma in Eastern and Southern Europe 1941-1944

Following the German invasion of the Soviet Union and Baltic states in 1941, Roma, like Jews, fell victim to mass killings perpetrated by SS-organised mobile killing squads. These squads, known as the *Einsatzgruppen*, followed the German Army as they advanced through the Soviet Union and the Soviet-controlled Baltic states, exterminating those they regarded as the Nazis' ideological or 'racial' enemies.

In other parts of eastern Europe and south-east Europe, such as Croatia, Hungary and Romania, fascist pro-Nazi regimes committed atrocities and mass murder against local Roma.

Many Roma victims of the genocide carried out by the Nazis and their collaborators were murdered in unrecorded killings, particularly those who died in Yugoslavia and the Soviet Union. This makes calculating the number of dead difficult. Recent research suggests that at least 220,000 and up to half-a-million Roma were murdered in the genocide, constituting perhaps a quarter or more of the Roma population of Europe.

Not only were killings unrecorded, but inaccurate census data makes it difficult to determine the size of the pre-war European Roma and Sinti community, and thus the numbers who perished.

Many hundreds of thousands of Roma survived arrests, deportations, camps and forced labour.

> ‘[The Crimchaks'] extermination along with the Jews proper and the gypsies in the Crimea was completed in the main by early December 1941. The fact that the Crimchaks and the gypsies shared the fate of the Jews did not arouse any special sensation among the population.’
>
> Extract from a Report from the Occupied Eastern Territories, submitted to the German Foreign Ministry in Berlin, 30 May 1942. Crimchaks are a Jewish ethno-religious community.

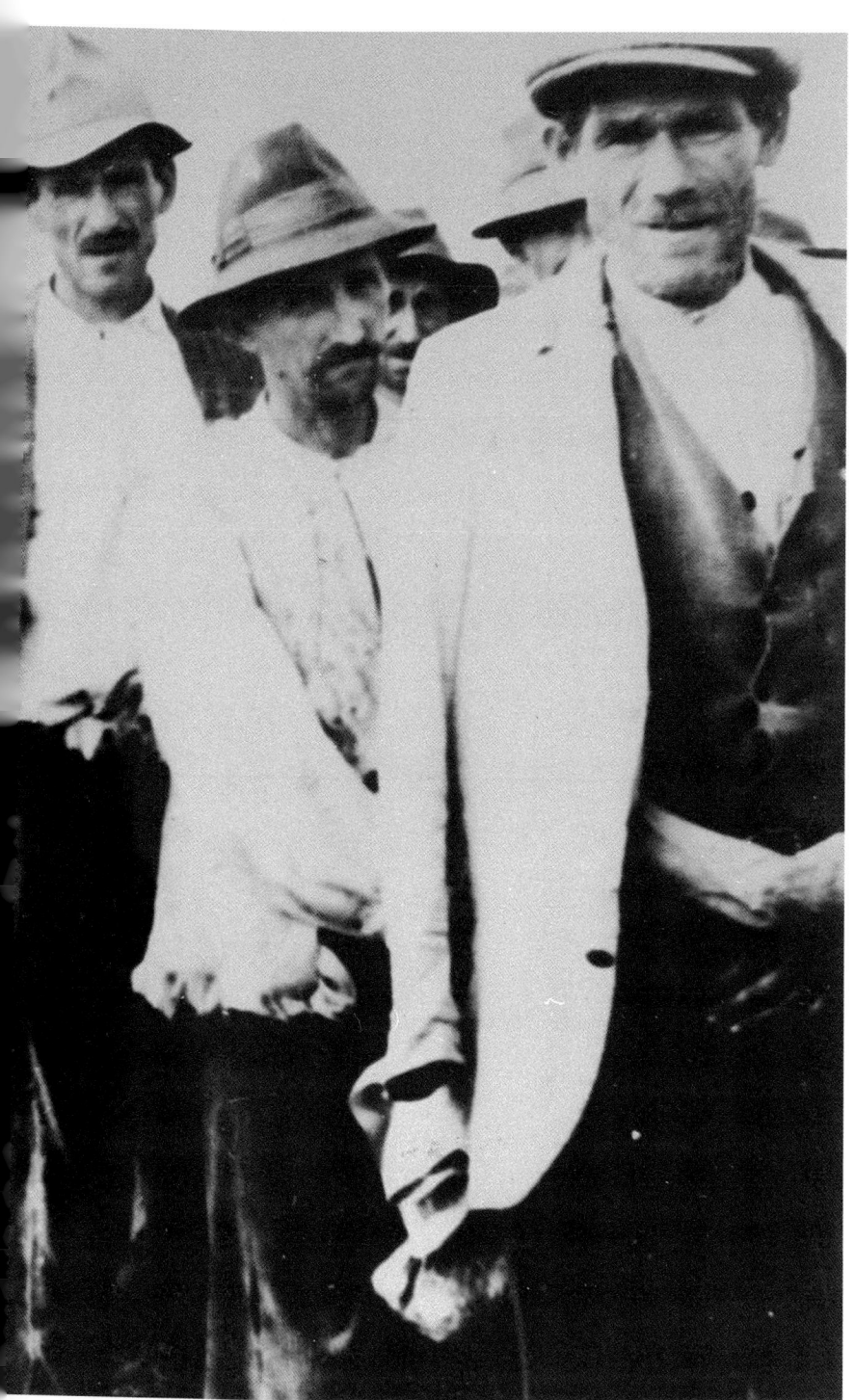

Roma and Serbs rounded up for deportation in Croatia, 1942
United States Holocaust Memorial Museum, courtesy of Muzej Revolucije Narodnosti Jugoslavije

08222

Wir Zigeuner appelieren an die zuständige Stelle, um uns zu unserem Recht zu verhelfen, das man uns ungerechter Weise vorenthalten will.

Wir wünschen, dass unsere Vertreter bei der zuständigen Stelle persönlich vorsprechen können.

Als unsere Vertreter fungieren :

Schneeberger Jakob, Wien XXI., Floridsdorferhauptstr. 12 und

F o y n Josef Wien XXI., Floridsdorferhauptstr. 12

Als Zeugen für unsere Angaben führen wir den letzten Lagerleiter Julius Brunner, Wien 18.,Bastiengasse Nr. 16/3.

Wir beglaubigen unsere Begründung mit den Unterschriften noch lebender ehemaliger Lagerinsaßen von Wien.

Josef Fojn — Katharina Held xxx — Weinrich, Rudolf
Wien 21, Hauptstr. 12 — Wien 21, Hauptstr. 12 — Wien 21, Arbeiterstrandbad str.

Mathias Weinrich +++ — Ludwig Weinrich +++
Wien 21, Bahndammweg N.5 — Wien 21, Bahn...

...mund Frost x+x — Theresia ...
Wien 21, Bahndammweg N. 12 — Arbeite...

...mil Weinrich ++x — Oskar Rosen...
Wien 21, Arbeiterstrand- badstraße N. 39a

Margaretha Held — Wien 21, Birnergasse N. 71

The post-war struggle for Recognition, Compensation and Justice

Across Europe since the post-war period, there has been scant recognition of the scale of the persecution of Roma communities that occurred during the Second World War.

Perpetrators were not prosecuted in war crimes trials for crimes against Romani individuals and communities. In Germany, restitution was initially denied to Roma and Sinti victims of Nazi persecution on the spurious grounds that they had not been targeted for racial reasons. In the Soviet Union and Communist Eastern Europe, the experiences of Roma during the genocide often went unacknowledged. There was little recognition of Roma as a group specifically targeted for persecution by the Nazis and their collaborators, and governments preferred to treat all as 'victims of fascist persecution' – which tended to mean that the suffering of marginalised Roma communities was ignored.

Since the war, Roma groups have campaigned for justice and memorialisation. Efforts have also been made by researchers to gather evidence of what had occurred.

In 1982, Germany officially recognised that genocide had been committed. The first apology from France for their collaboration in Nazi crimes against Roma and Sinti occurred in 2016.

The ongoing marginalisation of Roma, Gypsy and Traveller groups in Europe means that the struggle for recognition of the genocide against Roma continues.

Document signed by Austrian Roma survivors of Lackenbach concentration camp, Vienna, 30 September 1952. This document highlights attempts by former inmates of Lackenbach to get compensation after the war. The group appointed two named people as their representatives in this matter.
International Tracing Service Archive, Wiener Holocaust Library Collections, documents 82342528 and 82342528

Margarete Kraus

Journalist Reimar Gilsenbach interviewed Margarete Kraus about her experiences of persecution in Ludwigslust in Eastern Germany in 1966, when the photograph below was likely taken.

Kraus, originally from Czechoslovakia, was deported with her family to Auschwitz in about 1943 when she was a teenager. There she experienced maltreatment and privation and contracted typhus. She was also subjected to forced medical experiments in Auschwitz. Her parents perished in Auschwitz, and she was later transferred to Ravensbrück concentration camp.

Margarethe Kraus's Auschwitz camp number is visible on her left forearm. ■

Margarete Kraus, a Czech Roma survivor, photographed after the war by Reimar Gilsenbach
Wiener Holocaust Library Collections

Riddles

What have tongues
but cannot talk?

What have legs
but cannot walk?

What have eyes
but cannot see?

What have arms
but can't hug me?

Shoes have tongues but cannot talk.

Needles have eyes but cannot see.

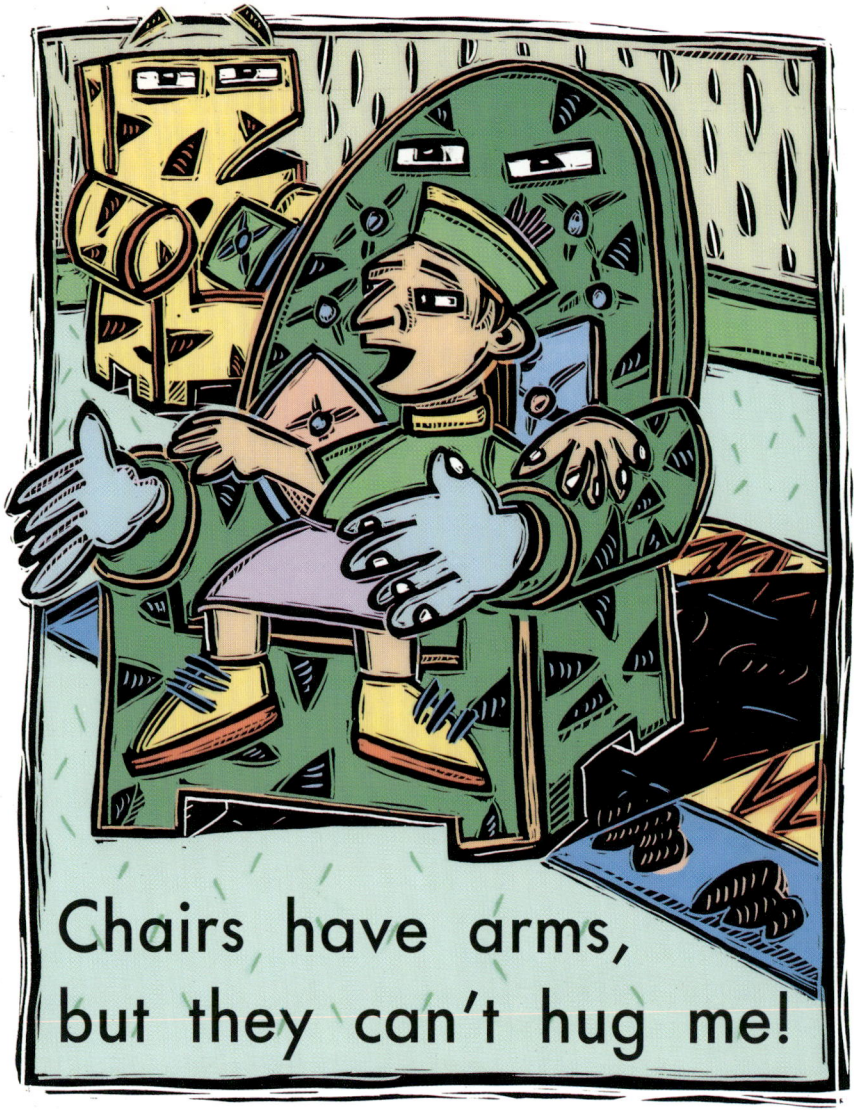

Chairs have arms, but they can't hug me!